TEACHER DEVELOPMENT RESOURCE

> Facilitation Notes precede each section

VERSUS
1	Native Speaker versus Non-Native Speaker	CDE
2	Classroom-based Researcher versus Struggling Teacher	ACD
3	Teaching Pronunciation versus Avoiding Pronunciation Work	CDE
4	Student versus Teacher	CDE

MY ACHIEVEMENTS AND CAPABILITIES
1	General	ACD
2	Teacher and Learner Roles	BCD

PROUD TO BE…
1	…a Non-Native Teacher!	CD
2	…a Native Speaking Teacher!	CD
3	…a Teacher!	ACD
4	…working in this School!	ACD

WAYS I CAN…
1	…make my life easier as a Teacher	ACD
2	…develop as a Teacher	ACD
3	…make my students more independent	CDE

INSECURITIES…
1	…Macro Skills	CDE
2	…Classroom Management	CD
3	…General	BCD

ADVISING…
1	…the Course Book Writer	BC
2	…the Principal	AC
3	…the Teacher	BC
4	…the Observer	AC

HOW TO…
1	…do your own Classroom Research	BCD
2	…encourage Learner Independence	BCDE
3	…cope with being observed	BCD

SMART ALEC…
1	Young Learners	CD
2	Equipment and Teaching Aids	CD
3	Introducing and practising New Language	CD
4	Various	CD

MY GOALS!
1	Teaching Reading and Listening	CDE
2	Professional – Short and Long Term	ACD

Key to Target group
- A   For Teachers of any subject
- B   Most of this material can be used with Teachers of any subject
- C   For Experienced Teachers
- D   For Inexperienced Teachers
- E   For Students as well as Teachers

English Experience, 25 Julian Road, Folkestone, Kent CT19 5HW

...VERSUS...

There are 4 **...VERSUS...** games

Aims
Game 1: To analyse and challenge the stereotypical images of **native and non-native speaker** teachers.
Game 2: To analyse and challenge the relevancy of **classroom-based research** for the teacher.
Game 3: To analyse and challenge the relevancy and practicality of focusing on **pronunciation** in the classroom.
Game 4: To analyse and challenge the attitudes of students and teachers towards the following everyday classroom situations and issues: a. **Independence**   b. **The target culture**   c. **L1 use**   d. **Classroom topics**

Instructions for all four of the **VERSUS** games are as follows:

Game Plan   Suggested timing: 30-40 minutes

– Participants divide into four groups: A, B, C, or D, and take the appropriate role card.

– Each group discusses its role and adds 3 other appropriate points to those already on the card.

– Form new groups to include one member from each of A,B,C,D.

– Argue your case so as to persuade the other participants that your view point is valid and justified.

❋ ❋ ❋ ❋ ❋ ❋

Variations

i) Use the role-cards as preparation stimulus for a formally organised debate.
   or
ii) Each person chooses a card which best describes their views and completes it with more points. The cards are then redistributed to other participants, who try to deduce the originator.
   or
iii) The session leader puts up the title of each **...Versus...** game. Participants brainstorm the possible arguments which each rolecard might contain and then check their predictions against the role cards.
   or
iv) Participants draft an article for their school newsletter or a professional journal, to highlight the main issues which affect their teaching situation.

TEACHER DEVELOPMENT RESOURCE BOOK

1:
NATIVE-SPEAKER *VERSUS* NON-NATIVE SPEAKER TEACHERS.

ROLE CARD A: NON-NATIVE SPEAKER.

You have realistic expectations of your students' needs and wants. You know the rules of English inside out, and can convey your excellent knowledge of the language in an accessible way. Your students know that you can really empathise with them, after all, you know what they're going through, you've been there yourself! You usually know exactly what mistakes your students will make.
On the back of this role card write 3 other reasons why it's great to be a non-native speaker teacher.

ROLE CARD B: NON-NATIVE SPEAKER.

You think that native speaker teachers are less committed to the profession. They usually begin to teach just so that they can earn money while travelling around the world. They don't care about testing and correction and let the students get away with murder.
You don't teach much cultural background to the language as 99% of your students will never set foot in the UK and are only studying English to pass school or university exams.
On the back of this role card write 3 other reasons why it's better not to be a native speaker teacher.

ROLE CARD C: NATIVE SPEAKER.

You are confident when you use English, but you think it's bad if students use their own language in class, and anyway, it makes you feel that you've lost control when the students start comparing English with a language that you don't understand very well. You give the students lots of cultural information about your own country. Even if they'll never go there, it's still important to learn about the culture that the language comes from. You stress communication over accuracy.
On the back of this role card write 3 other reasons why it's great to be a native speaker teacher.

ROLE CARD D: NATIVE SPEAKER.

You think that non-native speakers usually lack confidence about using English, and are too strict with their students to compensate for this. You don't think they should attempt to teach pronunciation. Also, they tend to overlook the informal, colloquial language. They don't use pair or group work much as they prefer the teacher-centred approach.
On the back of this role card write 3 other reasons why it's better not to be a non-native speaker teacher:

...VERSUS...

English Experience, 25 Julian Road, Folkestone, Kent CT19 5HW

TEACHER DEVELOPMENT RESOURCE BOOK

2:
CLASSROOM-BASED RESEARCHER *VERSUS* STRUGGLING TEACHER

ROLE CARD A: CLASSROOM-BASED RESEARCHER.

Classroom-based research has made you a better teacher with more satisfied students. It shows that you know **what** you are doing in class and **why**. In addition, it has made the students more aware of how they learn and developed their autonomy. You develop your creativity and time management skills through the way you integrate all the data collection into your normal teaching schedule.

It has also increased your status within the school. It has given you another string to your bow, and is the first step towards you becoming a teacher trainer, materials writer or researcher in the future.

On the back of this role card write 3 other reasons why you think it's <u>great</u> to do classroom-based research.

ROLE CARD B: CLASSROOM-BASED RESEARCHER.

Teachers who do not do classroom-based research view teaching merely as a nine-to-five job rather than as a high level profession. Their teaching is made up of stagnated, fossilised routines. They always do the same old thing in the classroom. Their Principal views them as complacent and dull. They do not keep up-to-date. They teach as prescribed by external bodies and cultures rather than by doing what is best for their students. Their students are disgruntled as they know that their needs are not being met.

On the back of this role card write 3 other reasons why you think it's <u>great to</u> do classroom-based research.

ROLE CARD C: STRUGGLING TEACHER.

You see classroom-based research as yet another passing fashion in ELT. You are not so gullible as to jump on every band wagon which comes along. You refuse to do classroom-based research as you know you teach well and have the certificate to prove your competence. You do not have to justify you actions in the classroom. You agree with the existing school syllabus and teaching policy. Your principal will not thank you for rocking the boat and breeding discontent among the students. You are already instinctively in touch with your learners and their needs. If it ain't broke; don't fix it!

On the back of this role card write 3 other reasons why you think it's <u>better not to do classroom-based research.</u>

ROLE CARD D: STRUGGLING TEACHER.

You would like to do classroom-based research but it is totally impossible. It involves unpaid time-consuming and labour intensive work. It yields results which cannot be generalised to other classes. Low level students get dissatisfied as you have to do the data collection activities with them in their L1. It is boring for the students and it is not what they are paying for. It leads students to then expect changes that may not be possible to make. It is like opening a can of worms. Presenting your results to your colleagues and the Principal is like showing everyone what you have been doing wrong all these years.

On the back of this role card write 3 other reasons why you think it's <u>better not to do classroom-based research.</u>

3: TEACHING PRONUNCIATION ...*VERSUS*... AVOIDING PRONUNCIATION WORK.

ROLE CARD A: PRONUNCIATION TEACHER.

Students expect and want to be taught pronunciation as part of their course. Teaching pronunciation allows students to see how comprehensible they are. It also helps them to understand native speakers and shows them all the different native speaker accents which exist. I raise students' confidence in their own pronunciation by getting them to act as models of correct pronunciation for the class. It shows the relationship between sounds and spelling in English.

It allows me to show students my expertise in an area that their previous teachers have not felt confident enough to deal with. I can integrate pronunciation work into my normal lesson. I can also use pronunciation activities to pad out my normal lessons or fill in time when I run out of materials.

On the back of this role card write 3 other reasons why it is good to teach pronunciation.

ROLE CARD B: PRONUNCIATION TEACHER.

Teachers who avoid pronunciation work are not really concerned about their students' needs. They show that they are only superficially concerned with their students' ability to communicate effectively. Teachers who avoid pronunciation activities look as if they do not know their subject – or are lazy! Students expect to cover pronunciation as part of the syllabus. Students will not thank you when they go abroad and find that they cannot understand or be understood. Students who have not had pronunciation work, can often only speak English with those who share their mother tongue accent! Avoiding pronunciation gives the false impression that either students are beyond hope or that they have great accents.

On the back of this role card write 3 other reasons why it is good to teach pronunciation.

ROLE CARD C: ANTI-PRONUNCIATION TEACHER.

There are no rules in pronunciation, only tendencies, so why bother? You cannot change a student's pronunciation in the long-term, especially when you are teaching adults. If teachers constantly pressurise students to achieve an impossible goal, they will destroy the students' confidence and de-motivate them.

Students should be encouraged to be proud of their foreign accents when they speak English. Your accent is an integral part of your identity. Students who attempt to loose their accent are ashamed of who they are. If students understand what they are saying and why, and say it with the appropriate emotion, then they will automatically use the appropriate intonation. All students pick up pronunciation naturally.

On the back of this role card write 3 other reasons why it is better not to teach pronunciation.

ROLE CARD D: ANTI-PRONUNCIATION TEACHER.

You would like to teach pronunciation but you have a multi-lingual class. No matter what you choose to focus on, it is bound to be irrelevant to someone. You do not know what accent to use as a standard model given the different needs of your students. You feel inferior and unqualified to teach pronunciation because you do not have an RP accent. The students get confused as you cannot seem to model the same intonation pattern twice! Pronunciation activities are totally uncommunicative, repetitive and boring and they embarrass adult students. All the 'arrows' and 'wavy lines' which are meant to mark intonation really confuse you.

On the back of this role card write 3 other reasons why it is better not to teach pronunciation.

TEACHER DEVELOPMENT RESOURCE BOOK

4:
STUDENT *VERSUS* TEACHER.

ROLE CARD A: STUDENT (I like what my teacher does. . .)

I feel in control and empowered in the classroom. My teacher shows that she values my knowledge by letting me teach the other students. The teacher credits me with the intelligence to work things out for myself.

In addition, I learn about the culture of countries where English is spoken.

I feel the teacher is giving me value for money as she only speaks English in class. My teacher encourages us to talk about a variety of things, so I also expand my general knowledge.

On the back of this role card write 3 other reasons why you <u>love</u> what the teacher does in class.

ROLE CARD B: STUDENT.(I'm not happy with what my teacher does . . .)

The teacher makes me do laborious, time-wasting exercises to find out the rules for myself. It is even worse when I ask a question and the teacher refuses to answer but tells me to "find out at home and present my findings to the whole class the next day". I am paying the teacher to teach, but she wants me to do her job for her!

The teacher also goes on about the "target culture" all the time. I am here to learn English, not to prepare to emigrate! The teacher spends ages giving lengthy, incomprehensible explanations and definitions in English when it would be more efficient to do that in my language. By the time the teacher has finished, I have forgotten what I was doing, or I have lost interest in it.

The teacher also expects us to discuss boring topics and then argues with us when we do not agree with her!

On the back of this role card write 3 other reasons why you <u>don't like</u> what the teacher does in class.

ROLE CARD C: TEACHER (I like what my students do in class. . .)

The students are great because they are mature enough to get on with things by themselves.

They love the target culture and show this in the way they lap up anything to do with English-language songs and movies.

Students get a real buzz out of successfully struggling to communicate only in English. My students add another dimension to my social life in the way we all chat together about topical social issues in class. They really expand my outlook on life.

On the back of this role card write 3 other reasons why you <u>like</u> what your students do in class.

ROLE CARD D: TEACHER (I'm unhappy with what my students do in class...)

Even though they are paying for the lessons, students do not try hard enough in class. They expect to be spoon-fed and are either apathetic or lack motivation.

They have a limited view of English culture. You cannot say you know the language if you do not know about the culture from which it comes.

Students use their own language in class all the time and spend half the lesson with their noses buried in their bilingual dictionaries.

They do not see English as a medium of normal communication. Students always say that they want to talk more in class, but they never have anything to say about social and political issues.

On the back of this role card write 3 other reasons why you <u>don't like</u> what your students do in class.

TEACHER DEVELOPMENT RESOURCE BOOK

There are 2 **Achievements and Capabilitie**s games. Game 1 is about professional life:– general; Game 2 works on Teacher and Learner Roles.

Instructions for both **MY ACHIEVEMENTS AND CAPABILITIES** games.

Game Plan   Suggested timing: 90 minutes
This is a four step activity.

A. Achievements

Complete an achievement sheet individually, listing the things done to date as a teacher (or student if applicable). Remember that even seemingly small achievements are important and relevant here.

In groups, compare and comment on these achievements, and provide background information on how and why these things occurred.

The group should offer ideas to help everyone complete all the sentences.

B. Well I Never…

Complete the **Well I Never…**sentences individually to summarise your reactions to colleagues' achievements.

Discuss these reactions and see whether what other people noted about the achievements were similar or dissimilar.

C. My Capabilities: I Could…

In groups again, each group completes the **I Could…** sentences according to what they feel capable of doing but haven't done yet.

Groups then exchange sheets. This new sheet is a list of possible things they could achieve.

Each group ranks the sentences from 1 (most practical) to 10 (least practical).

Groups then report back to the class on the reasons for their ranking.

At the end, each participant takes one of the **I Could…** sentences (from any group in the class) and resolves to achieve it during the next two weeks/ term.

D. The Steps I'd Have To Take

Participants join together with those who have chosen similar sentences (or in random pairs) to complete the list of steps thought necessary in order to achieve their chosen goal.

Report back on whether in the light of close scrutiny, the target is realistically achievable or not.

If it wasn't thought to be realistic, the class suggests how it could be adapted to become more attainable.

* * * * * *

Variations
i)   Less experienced teachers can omit stages A and B. Instead, they can focus on stages C and D to explore their future potential.

or

ii) In groups, participants can choose to focus on other areas related to teaching, e.g. skills; pronunciation; vocabulary; motivation; classroom management etc. They should then devise a set of A and B game sheets. Groups exchange these, try them out, and evaluate them for relevancy, appropriacy to the topic, and the extent to which they raised the participants awareness of the chosen area.

TEACHER DEVELOPMENT RESOURCE BOOK

1:
GENERAL

Aims:
    To raise teachers' awareness as to what they have already achieved in their professional life.
    To give teachers recognition for these achievements.
    To encourage teachers to expand on these achievements.
    To help teachers break down goals into manageable steps.

A. ACHIEVEMENTS. I HAVE...
1. trained ....
2. taught ....
3. developed ....
4. counselled ....
5. networked ....
6. overseen ....
7. organised ....
8. implemented ....
9. consolidated ....
10. lectured ....

* * * * * *

B. WELL I NEVER...
1. I was surprised at ....
2. I was impressed by ....
3. I found it hard to believe that ....
4. I wish I could also have ....
5. The teacher must have been crazy to have ....

* * * * * *

                                                                    Roles I'd like to introduce.
                                                                    Prioritise 3 of them.

C. MY CAPABILITIES: I COULD...
1. train ....
2. teach ....
3. develop ....
4. counsel ....
5. network ....
6. oversee ....
7. organise ....
8. implement ....
9. consolidate ....
10. lecture ....

The goal I have chosen is ....

Time scale for achieving this ....

* * * * * *

D. The steps I'd have to take

....
....
....

MY ACHIEVEMENTS AND CAPABILITIES

English Experience, 25 Julian Road, Folkestone, Kent CT19 5HW

TEACHER DEVELOPMENT RESOURCE BOOK

2: TEACHER AND LEARNER ROLES.

Aims:
To raise awareness of the variety of professional roles teachers have already played..
To give teachers recognition for these achievements.
To encourage teachers to expand on the roles that they and their learners play.
To help teachers break down goals into manageable steps.

A. ROLES I HAVE PERFORMED.   I WAS A/AN...
1. guide when I
2. involver when I
3. diagnostician when I
4. arbitrator when I
5. counsellor when I
6. entertainer when I
7. inhibitor when I
8. police officer when I
9. nagger when I
10. mother when I
11. lecturer when I
12. walking dictionary when I

* * * * * *

B. WELL I NEVER..!
1. I was surprised at
2. I was impressed by
3. I wish I could also have
4. The teacher must have been crazy to have

Roles I'd like to introduce.
Prioritise 3 of them.

* * * * * *

C. CAPABILITIES: I COULD ENCOURAGE MY STUDENTS TO BE...
1. researchers if they
2. teachers if they
3. monitors if they
4. materials writers if they
5. rule-setters if they
6. counsellors if they
7. negotiators if they
8. sponges if they
9. organisers if they
10. providers if they
11. goal-setters if they
12. motivators if they
13. performers if they
14. artists if they
15. achievers if they

The goal I have chosen is ....

Time scale for achieving this ....

* * * * * *

D. The steps I'd have to take

MY ACHIEVEMENTS AND CAPABILITIES

English Experience, 25 Julian Road, Folkestone, Kent CT19 5HW

TEACHER DEVELOPMENT RESOURCE BOOK

There are 4 **PROUD TO BE...** games.

Aims

1: To raise awareness of the advantages of being a non-native speaker teacher.
   To analyse the attitudes and misconceptions behind the native speaker/ non-native speaker distinction.
2: To raise awareness of the advantages of being a native speaker teacher.
   To analyse the attitudes and misconceptions behind the native speaker/ non-native speaker distinction.
3: To raise awareness of the advantages of being a teacher.
   To analyse the attitudes and misconceptions behind the critics and supporters of the profession.
4: To raise awareness of the advantages of the teachers' working environment.
   To analyse the teachers' perceptions of the place in which they work.

Instructions/Game Plan   Suggested timing: 30-40 minutes

i) Cut out the cards. Participants take 4 cards each, and consider to what extent each of the statements is true in relation to their own particular teaching situation.

ii) They mingle in order to swap their cards for four new cards which better apply to their working lives.

iii) They form groups to describe and justify why they chose their new cards.

* * * * * *

Variations

i) Participants divide the statement cards into two piles according to those which specific categories of people would agree or disagree with; e.g. native speaker teachers and non-native speaker teachers; principals and teachers; students and teachers etc. Use previous experience to justify these decisions.

or

ii) Participants individually sort the cards into four piles as follows:

DESIRABLE – and TRUE FOR MY TEACHING SITUATION	NOT DESIRABLE – but TRUE FOR MY TEACHING SITUATION
NOT DESIRABLE – and FALSE FOR MY TEACHING SITUATION	DESIRABLE – but FALSE FOR MY TEACHING SITUATION

- Participants then compare and justify their groupings. (Participants from the same teaching environment can do this to see the extent to which they share the same perception of their working environment and teaching situation.)

- Each group of participants ranks a number of these cards in one of the following ways: applicable – irrelevant; desirable – undesirable; true – false; native speaker – non-native speaker.

- Groups leave their final ranking on their table and swap places with another group in order to evaluate **their** ranking. They should **change it** if they disagree but a group secretary must note any changes made. This rotation can take place several times until all participants have seen all the sets of ranked cards. The class can then compare and justify the main changes they made to other groups' rankings.

1:
PROUD TO BE A NON-NATIVE SPEAKER TEACHER!

I'm bilingual, whereas most native speakers aren't.	I focus more on grammatical accuracy than native speakers.	My employer doesn't need to make visa/work permit arrangements for me.
I can impress people socially by casually interweaving English expressions into my party chit-chat.	I can mix methodology from native-speaker education systems with those of my own country.	I can mix methodology from native-speaker education systems with those of my own country.
Unlike native speakers, I know a lot about successful strategies for learning English.	I'm living proof for my students that proficiency in English is an attainable and worthwhile goal.	I'm stricter on spelling accuracy than native speakers.
I know my student's culture better than a native speaker does.	I can give students more information about the English language than native speakers.	I can use the student's L1 in class to translate and explain, whereas native speakers can't.
I'm better with low levels than native speakers are.	For me, teaching is a career, whereas for a native speaker, it's a chance to see a new country.	I know the way students expect to be taught better than a native speaker does.
I'm cheaper than a native speaker.	The school is obliged to send me to English-speaking environments for refresher training.	I can easily work in state school in my country, whereas a native speaker can't.
I can accurately predict what errors students will make and why, whereas native speakers can't.	I understand my students' motivations for learning English better than a native speaker does.	

PROUD TO BE...

TEACHER DEVELOPMENT RESOURCE BOOK

2: PROUD TO BE A NATIVE SPEAKER TEACHER!

PROUD TO BE...

- I perform an ambassadorial role when I work abroad.
- Non-native teachers use me to improve their English.
- I am treated as a methodology expert when I work abroad.
- I motivate students by my presence.

- When I teach abroad, students feel privileged that I've come all that way to teach them.
- I can create the environment of the target culture when I'm abroad.
- I'm more spontaneous and flexible than a non-native speaker teacher.
- I can get a better position than a non-native speaker teacher regardless of qualifications and experience.

- I teach not only the language but the culture too.
- I approach language as a communicative medium rather than as an academic subject to be learnt.
- I have a gut feeling about what's right in English.
- I can get a job in any country in the world.

- No-one expects me to learn the students' L1.
- I motivate students to negotiate meaning.
- I provide more opportunities for authentic communication because I don't know the students' L1 well.
- Students speak more in classrooms with a native speaker teacher.

- I can get a Teacher Training position more easily than a non-native speaker teacher.
- I'm more confident with higher levels than non-native speaker teachers.
- I do more pronunciation work than non-native speaker teachers.
- I'm a better pronunciation model than non-native speaker teachers.

TEACHER DEVELOPMENT RESOURCE BOOK

There are 3 **Ways I Can...** games

Aim for Game 1: To explore ways of making the teacher's life easier.
Aim for Game 2: To explore ways that teachers can help their students to be more independent.
Aim for Game 3: To explore the various means of professional development for teachers.

The Game Plan is the same for each.   Suggested timing: 50-60 minutes

List A.
   Participants form pairs or groups to complete list A with ideas on how they could change aspects of their lives as teachers.
   Participants then swap sheets with another pair or group and circle the 3 best ideas on their new sheet.
   The class then evaluates them and comments on the feasibility of implementing them.

List B.
   In groups or pairs, participants score the suggestions from 5 (the most attractive) to 1 (the least attractive).
   Participants then choose the top 3 most attractive and the bottom 3 least attractive, and justify their choice to another group or pair.

✶ ✶ ✶ ✶ ✶ ✶

Variations

i) Pairs of participants complete list A in the manner of one of the following roles:

A teacher at a small, budget school;   A teacher at a large, no-expenses-spared school;   A teacher at a traditional, staid, no-risks school;   A teacher at an experimental, forward-thinking school.

Participants with the same role card then get together to plan and deliver a workshop presentation to convince the other groups of the validity of their ideas. As each group present their ideas, the other groups take notes on the points and ideas that they agree and disagree with. After the presentations, each group prepares a summarised evaluation of the other groups' presentations. The class can then discuss and evaluate the points raised in each presentation in the light of their own teaching experience.

or

ii) Participants rank the suggestions on list B in the manner of their role above. They then mingle with other participants to compare and justify their rankings in the manner of their role.

or

iii) Individually, participants complete list A in the manner of one of the roles above, (or according to their own teaching situation). Participants then form pairs and go through the list, trying to predict the way in which their partner has completed each sentence. One point is given for each correct answer.

or

iv) Participants can mark the statements in list B, **True** or **False** according to their own teaching situation. They can then mingle to find someone who has marked **True** for a statement which they themselves have marked **False**. The person who has marked the statement as **True**, should explain their experience in relation to this, and give helpful and practical tips on how it can be implemented successfully.

English Experience, 25 Julian Road, Folkestone, Kent CT19 5HW

TEACHER DEVELOPMENT RESOURCE BOOK

1: WAYS I CAN MAKE MY LIFE EASIER AS A TEACHER.

LIST A

I could change ....

I could pilfer ....

I could laminate ....

I could start ....

I could put up ....

I could regularly swap ....

I could make ....

I could cut down ....

I could get students to ....

I could stimulate ....

❉ ❉ ❉ ❉ ❉ ❉

WAYS I CAN MAKE MY LIFE EASIER AS A TEACHER.

LIST B   Score these from 5 (very attractive option) to 1 (unattractive option)

Change schools.
Take a stress management course.
Pilfer inconsequential school materials.
Laminate my favourite activity cards and sheets to cut down on pre-lesson cut-and-stick time.
Start peer-correction of homework.
Be organised by putting running order of the contents/activities of the lesson on the board
Respond to difficult questions by politely stalling until I find the answer.
Regularly swap supplementary materials with other teachers of similar classes.
Make a photo collage which reflects the way I want others to perceive me. Study it every day.
Cut down my number of school classes and do more private work instead.
Get one half of the class to write the progress tests for the other half of the class.
Get a student to operate the tape and video.
Stimulate peer correction and explanation.
Have a pair/group of students prepare and teach a pre-set teaching point each week.

My top 3 Action options are   ....

....

....

TEACHER DEVELOPMENT RESOURCE BOOK

2:   WAYS I CAN HELP MY STUDENTS TO BE MORE INDEPENDENT.

LIST A

The classroom materials could be ....

The tests could be ....

The classroom activities could be ....

Language presentations could be ....

Dictionaries could be ....

Class outings to films could be used to..

Students could help each other to..

The self-access centre could ....

I could abdicate ....

* * * * * *

WAYS I CAN HELP MY STUDENTS TO BE MORE INDEPENDENT.

LIST B   *Score these from 5 (very attractive option) to 1 (unattractive option)*

   Base all classroom activities on materials that students have provided themselves.
   Get one half of the class to write progress tests for the other half of the class.
   Abandon teacher presentations. Make the students peer-teachers.
   Avoid correction and explanation by the teacher.
   Get groups to choose a text and prepare reading tasks for the class.
   Have monthly class meetings to set and discuss home-study goals.
   Do project work which involves the students in utilising the English resources in their community.
   Teach a variety of study strategies and dictionary skills.
   Have students set their own daily homework tasks.
   Encourage class subscriptions to an English language newspaper or magazine.
   Make book reports an integral part of the assessment system.
   Have task-related class outings to English language films or theatre productions.
   Pair students with a study partner.
   Ensure that student-made activity sheets are an integral part of the self-access centre.

My top 3 Action options are   ....

....

....

English Experience, 25 Julian Road, Folkestone, Kent CT19 5HW

TEACHER DEVELOPMENT RESOURCE BOOK

3: WAYS I CAN DEVELOP AS A TEACHER.

LIST A

I could carry out ....

I could write and distribute ....

I could tape ....

I could become an apprentice to ....

I could evaluate ....

I could study ....

I could chair ....

I could send off ....

I could apply for ....

I could observe ....

I could peer- ....

❉ ❉ ❉ ❉ ❉

WAYS I CAN DEVELOP AS A TEACHER.

LIST B   *Score these from 5 (very attractive option) to 1 (unattractive option)*

Carry out action research to find the causes of a common classroom problem.

Teach a lesson using a new technique to two different classes and evaluate the responses

Circulate a Questionnaire to investigate teachers' attitudes to some classroom problems. Arrange a staff meeting to discuss the findings and propose solutions.

Arrange peer-observations with a teacher who you like and trust.

Set up a course book evaluation and supplementation workshop.

Initiate an apprentice and mentor programme.

Regularly video or audio tape parts of your lessons.

Initiate a system for evaluating every worksheet photocopied by teachers.

Take a part-time or distance learning teaching qualification.

Arrange a weekly peer-lesson planning rota.

Encourage teachers to contribute to a weekly list of action points to be discussed at staff meetings.

Arrange for a rota of different teachers to chair staff meetings.

Arrange for pre- and post-lesson evaluative discussions with a senior teacher or teacher trainer.

Watch and discuss a segment of a teaching video with your colleagues.

Arrange a Materials Night for every teacher to bring an original classroom activity that they have made.

Start a regular discussion Group in which each teacher summarises an interesting article.

Start a teachers' newsletter and circulate it to other schools in your area.

Set up in-service Teacher Development sessions to be jointly planned and facilitated.

My top 3 Action options are   ....

....

....

English Experience, 25 Julian Road, Folkestone, Kent CT19 5HW

TEACHER DEVELOPMENT RESOURCE BOOK

There are 4 **Insecurities about...** games

Aims

Game 1: To encourage teachers to share their attitudes and difficulties relating to *teaching listening, speaking, reading and writing*.

Game 2: To encourage teachers to share their attitudes and difficulties relating to *classroom management*.

Game 3: To encourage teachers to share their attitudes and difficulties relating to the *correction of spoken and written errors*.

Game 4: To encourage teachers to share their *professional problems*.

Instructions for all the Insecurities about... games   Suggested timing: 40-50 minutes

In groups, each participant picks a card from the pile. Allow a few minutes 'thinking time' and then participants describe a teaching situation (real or imaginary) related to it.

The other group members ask the speaker questions and try to guess whether it's the truth or a mere fabrication!

✱ ✱ ✱ ✱ ✱ ✱

Variations

i) Each participants has a set of cards and divides them into two piles:

Pile 1: Problems that I'm not sure how to deal with.
Pile 2: Problems that I could deal with.

Participants mingle in order to find someone who can offer suggestions on how to deal with any of the problems that they have placed in the first pile. When they find a satisfactory or helpful suggestion, they should transfer that card from Pile 1 to Pile 2. The class can then discuss any problems which still remain.

or

ii) In groups, participants discuss in order to arrange the cards under the following headings:

A non-native speaker teacher's problems / A native speaker teacher's problems;   A state school teacher's problems / A private school teacher's problems;   An inexperienced teacher's problems / An experienced teacher's problems.

Participants can then compare and justify their decisions with those of the other groups.

or

iii) Each participant chooses a card which describes a problem that they have recently experienced. They attach their card to a large piece of paper and write their initials on it. They then give it to another participant, who writes a suggestion or solution to this problem on the paper. All the papers/cards circulate for further suggestions to be written down. At the end, participants re-claim their original pieces of paper, choose which piece of advice they like best and share what they have learned.

English Experience, 25 Julian Road, Folkestone, Kent CT19 5HW

TEACHER DEVELOPMENT RESOURCE BOOK

1: INSECURITIES ABOUT MACRO SKILLS

INSECURITIES...

I just muddled through skills work as I didn't know how to approach it well.	I was testing listening rather than teaching it.	I didn't use songs as they don't teach proper English.	I didn't teach reading. I just taught vocabulary set in a text.
My students complained about having to write in pairs and groups.	I couldn't get students to accept authentic listening texts which had background noise and mumbling speakers.	I INSISTED that students understood every single word of a listening or reading text.	The speaking task was so intrinsically motivating that students used their L1 to complete it.
I let the male students dominate in speaking activities.	I only used authentic reading texts with advanced students and not with other levels.	In writing activities, I focused on grammatical and lexical accuracy at the expense of organisation, planning and creativity	Process writing didn't work in my classroom.
My students translated as they read.	My students wrote in the L1 first, then translated it.	Discussion activities proved to be a waste of time considering how little the students learnt from them.	Students weren't allowed to write the new language until they could use the language accurately when they spoke.

2: INSECURITIES ABOUT CLASSROOM MANAGEMENT

I felt like a police officer or a baby sitter.	The silence in the classroom worried me.	I got angry and a bit upset.	In class discussions, students looked at me for permission to speak.
I repeated or reformulated my instruction immediately.	I didn't know what I should do when monitoring.	My bad timing messed up the whole lesson.	My students refused to take more responsibility and be more independent in the classroom.
I had my favourite students, and the rest of the class knew it.	I felt stupid doing the mimes and gestures that teachers are meant to use.	I couldn't keep the whole class' attention.	I couldn't remember students' names.
My students didn't want to do pair or group work.	I felt that a teacher couldn't talk too much in the target language.	'Eliciting' was 'like pulling teeth'.	I blamed the students for my failure to establish rapport.

TEACHER DEVELOPMENT RESOURCE BOOK

3: INSECURITIES ABOUT ERRORS

INSECURITIES...

The more I corrected, the less the students spoke.	I made sure my students knew it was bad to make mistakes.	My students made a lot of errors and I felt I'd failed.	I corrected a student wrongly and they knew that I had.
A student checked my vocabulary correction in the dictionary in front of me.	I was paid to make sure that the students didn't make mistakes when they spoke.	My students complained over the amount I corrected them.	Students errors irritated me.
I constantly interrupted students to correct errors.	I didn't write students' errors on the board in case they picked up bad habits.	Contrastive analysis between the L1 and the L2 was damaging and unhelpful.	Errors were just the manifestation of laziness.
I constantly interrupted students to correct errors.	I corrected all written errors and highlighted them with red pen.	I humiliated or embarrassed a student who had made a mistake.	Students thought that I encouraged them to correct each other because I didn't know the answer myself!

4: GENERAL INSECURITIES

I talked so much that the students hardly had a chance to open their mouths!	The school seemed to be getting worse.	I felt native speaker teachers were better than non-native speaker teachers.	
I lost control of a kids' class.	I preferred not to be a Director of Studies, as I was afraid I might hurt someone.	A non-native speaker teacher was afraid to tell a native speaker that she didn't understand what had been said.	
I avoided pair/group work as I was afraid of losing control of the class.	Teaching just seemed like a lot of hard work.	Teaching was neither noble or spiritual.	I didn't feel my teaching was improving.
I felt unconfident about teaching a high level class for the first time.	I felt uneasy about discussing my teaching problems in the staffroom.	I didn't feel in control of my career.	I haven't been able to go abroad for various reasons, and this has held me back as a teacher.

TEACHER DEVELOPMENT RESOURCE BOOK

There are 4 **Advising . . .** games. The aims are

Game 1: To raise teacher's awareness of the processes involved in *materials production*.
Game 2: To raise teacher's awareness of the role of *management* in schools.
Game 3: To raise teacher's awareness of the *needs and wants* of their students.
Game 4: To raise teacher's awareness of the role of the *classroom observer*.

For all the **Advising...** games.

Game Plan. Suggested timing: 60 minutes

i) **Role Cards:**
Participants form 4 groups. Each group is assigned one of the role cards. (N.B. In **Advising 1: Advising the Course Book Writer**, participants with role cards C or D should insert the name of a course book they are familiar with.)

ii) **First Discussion**
Each group discusses and answers the 12 questions *in the style of their role*.
Each group member needs to make notes for the next stage of the activity.

The Meeting – Proposals:
Participants form new groups, containing one member from each of the previous groups, to hold a meeting.
Each member of the group (in role as A B C or D) puts his/her point of view on the 12 discussion points.
The group then collectively agrees and notes a proposal / position in response to each discussion point.
The class compares and evaluates the proposals made by each group.

✼ ✼ ✼ ✼ ✼ ✼

Variation
Participants draw up their own lists of questions to be raised at the meeting and then compare it with the list given below. They then discuss the relevance of the questions given to their own teaching situations.

English Experience, 25 Julian Road, Folkestone, Kent CT19 5HW

TEACHER DEVELOPMENT RESOURCE BOOK

1: *ADVISING THE COURSE BOOK WRITER.*
Role cards.

First Discussion		The Meeting (Note any agreed proposals)
Question 1. Answers	Why do course book writers use non-authentic texts?	1 –
Question 2. Answers	Why don't the teacher's books contain a variety of extra supplementary activities?	2 –
Question 3. Answers	Why don't course books say how long each activity will take?	3 –
Question 4. Answers	Why aren't more controversial topics focused on?	4 –
Question 5. Answers	Why aren't there more information gap games in the course books?	5 –
Question 6. Answers	How do course book writers arrive at an approach and method on which to base the material?	6 –
Question 7. Answers	How is the type of course book syllabus (e.g. lexical, grammatical, mixed etc.) chosen?	7 –
Question 8. Answers	To what extent do course book-led classes ignore the needs and wants of the individual student?	8 –
Question 9. Answers	How can course books be used by students when they study independently?	9 –
Question 10. Answers	To what extent are the teachers' books of course books expected to be idiot-proof?	10 –
Question 11. Answers	Why do course books contain so few tests?	11 –
Question 12. Answers	How do course books teach the students how to learn?	12 –

a.) You are a "COURSE BOOK DEPENDENT" TEACHER

b.) You are an "ANTI-COURSE BOOK" TEACHER

c.) You are the "WRITER OF a COURSE BOOK"

d.) You are the "WRITER OF a COURSE BOOK"

ADVISING...

English Experience, 25 Julian Road, Folkestone, Kent CT19 5HW

TEACHER DEVELOPMENT RESOURCE BOOK

2: ADVISING THE PRINCIPAL.
Role cards.

First Discussion		The Meeting (Note any agreed proposals)
Question 1. Answers	How often does the principal have one-to-one chats with the teachers? Why?	1 –
Question 2. Answers	How does the principal show a commitment to improving the quality of teaching?	2 –
Question 3. Answers	How does the principal develop a positive school atmosphere?	3 –
Question 4. Answers	What criteria should be used to select a new teacher?	4 –
Question 5. Answers	What training does the principal give the teachers?	5 –
Question 6. Answers	What training does the principal have?	6 –
Question 7. Answers	How are the teachers rewarded?	7 –
Question 8. Answers	How does the principal ensure punctuality?	8 –
Question 9. Answers	What occasions does the principal celebrate at school?	9 –
Question 10. Answers	What changes do you want to take place in the school in the next year?	10 –
Question 11. Answers	How does the principal find out what the teachers think?	11 –
Question 12. Answers	How does the principal find out what the students think about the teaching?	12 –

a.) You are the

"PRINCIPAL FROM HELL"

b.) You are the "DOWNTRODDEN,

GRUMPY TEACHER"

c.) You are the

"DREAM PRINCIPAL"

d.) You are the

"AMBITIOUS TEACHER"

ADVISING...

English Experience, 25 Julian Road, Folkestone, Kent CT19 5HW

TEACHER DEVELOPMENT RESOURCE BOOK

3: ADVISING THE TEACHER.
Role cards.

First Discussion	The Meeting (Note any agreed proposals)
Question 1. To what extent does the teacher negotiate the syllabus with the students? **Answers**	1 –
Question 2. What opportunities do students have to talk to the teacher about their learning difficulties? **Answers**	2 –
Question 3. To what extent is the rationale for the teaching approach made explicit to the students? **Answers**	3 –
Question 4. When do the students have the opportunity to select reading texts? **Answers**	4 –
Question 5. How does the teacher monitor and act on students' problem areas? **Answers**	5 –
Question 6. What feedback procedures are in place to allow students to report on the effectiveness and efficiency of their teacher? **Answers**	6 –
Question 7. How often do the students see their records and discuss them with their teacher? **Answers**	7 –
Question 8. What measures are taken to discover the students' preferred learning styles and strategies? **Answers**	8 –
Question 9. To what extent are students involved in decisions concerning school and class resources? **Answers**	9 –
Question 10. How are the needs and wants of the individual catered for in group classes? **Answers**	10 –
Question 11. What constraints prevent the classroom from being a learner-centred environment? **Answers**	11 –
Question 12. How is student solidarity and interdependence be fostered? **Answers**	12 –

a.) You are the "TEACHER FROM HELL"

b.) You are the "DOWNTRODDEN, GRUMPY STUDENT"

c.) You are the "DREAM TEACHER"

d.) You are the "MOTIVATED, CHIRPY STUDENT"

ADVISING…

English Experience, 25 Julian Road, Folkestone, Kent CT19 5HW

TEACHER DEVELOPMENT RESOURCE BOOK

4: ADVISING THE OBSERVER.
Role cards.

First Discussion		The Meeting (Note any agreed proposals)
Question 1.	Why can't the teacher observe the observer teaching?	1 –
Answers		
Question 2.	How often should the observer plan the lesson with the teacher?	2 –
Answers		
Question 3.	How does the teacher's dress and appearance affect the observer's judgement?	3 –
Answers		4 –
Question 4.	How can the observer win the teacher's trust and confidence?	
Answers		5 –
Question 5.	How does the presence of an observer affect the performance of the students?	
Answers		6 –
Question 6.	What are the three top sins that observers criticise teachers for?	
Answers		7 –
Question 7.	What kind of lesson plan do observers expect to be given before the observation?	
Answers		8 –
Question 8.	How should the post-observation chat be conducted?	
Answers		9 –
Question 9.	How should the teacher give feedback on the observers' effectiveness?	
Answers		10 –
Question 10.	What action should the observer take on the basis of the observation?	
Answers		11 –
Question 11.	How often should teachers be observed?	
Answers		12 –
Question 12.	How similar are teachers' observed lessons to what they normally do in class?	
Answers		

a.) You are the "SENSITIVE AND AUTHORITY- WARY TEACHER"

b.) You are the "CRITICAL AND TRADITIONAL OBSERVER"

c.) You are the "ASSURED AND EXPERIMENTAL TEACHER"

d.) You are the "EMPATHETIC AND PROGRESSIVE OBSERVER"

ADVISING...

English Experience, 25 Julian Road, Folkestone, Kent CT19 5HW

TEACHER DEVELOPMENT RESOURCE BOOK

There are 3 **How to...** games

The aims are:
Game 1: To demystify **classroom research** and encourage teachers to share their own experiences.
Game 2: To encourage teachers to evaluate the way they approach **learner independence**.
Game 3: To help teachers cope with the potentially stressful situation of **being observed.**

Instructions for all **How to...** games.

Game Plan   Suggested timing 50-60 minutes
Participants divide into two groups.
Group A notes the possible advantages of each piece of advice.
Group B notes the possible disadvantages.
Participants re-form into new groups containing representatives from A and B. They evaluate the advantages and disadvantages listed, and score the pieces of advice from each section **a), b)** or **c)** from the **most** to the **least** practical.
The groups then add their own advice to each section, and justify this advice to the class.

※ ※ ※ ※ ※ ※

Variations
i) Individually, participants first compile their own lists of advice. They then form groups to share, discuss and evaluate each others' suggestions. The participants then compare their advice with that given on the game sheets.

or

ii) Each group of participants evaluates the advice from a different standpoint, for example, *an inexperienced teacher; a young learner; an adult student; a state school teacher; a private school teacher; a one-to-one teacher; a school principal etc.*

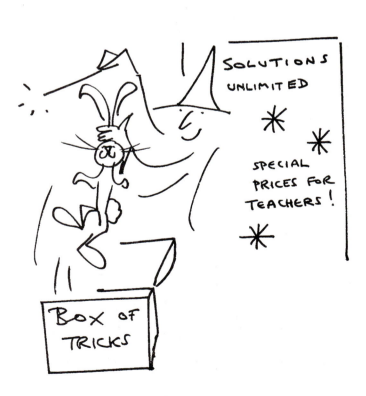

English Experience, 25 Julian Road, Folkestone, Kent CT19 5HW

TEACHER DEVELOPMENT RESOURCE BOOK

1: DO YOUR OWN CLASSROOM RESEARCH.

Group A note advantages
Group b note disadvantages

Score (a–c)

a) Identifying the area to be researched.
    Advice

1. Study Video or audio tapes of your students.
2. Give students a list of potential research areas to discuss and rank.
3. Give the students the responsibility of deciding on the area to be researched.
4. Discuss the possible areas to be researched with other teachers and the principal.
5. Have another teacher or the principal observe the class and set your research area for you.

My 'best advice': 1. ....

2. ....

✻ ✻ ✻ ✻ ✻ ✻

Group A note advantages
Group b note disadvantages

Score (a–c)

b) Collecting the Data.
    Advice

1. Integrate the data collection into the normal lesson, e.g. through class discussion of the area being researched.
2. Design questionnaires.
3. Install a suggestion box.
4. Students prepare and give a presentation on the research area in order to propose solutions and changes.
5. Learners keep diaries observing the research area.
6. Students role play situations which highlight the problem.
7. Interview individual students.
8. Gather data from other classes too.

My 'best advice': 1. ....

2. ....

✻ ✻ ✻ ✻ ✻ ✻

Group A note advantages
Group b note disadvantages

Score (a–c)

c) Analysing the Data and Taking Action.
    Advice

1. Make a graph or a chart.
2. Use numerical statistics and percentages.
3. Write a report.
4. Submit your findings to the principal.
5. Present your findings at a staff meeting.
6. Write an article for an ELT publication.
7. Get sponsored to give a presentation at an ELT conference.
8. Have students tabulate and analyse the data.
9. Have students propose solutions and vote for the most popular.
10. Do extensive background reading on your research area.

My 'best advice': 1. ....

2. ....

English Experience, 25 Julian Road, Folkestone, Kent CT19 5HW

TEACHER DEVELOPMENT RESOURCE BOOK

2: ENCOURAGE LEARNER INDEPENDENCE.

Group A note advantages
Group b note disadvantages
Score (a–c)

a) **Degrees of learner independence.** The student . . .

1. selects what is to be learned.
2. identifies own needs.
3. selects the teaching materials.
4. is responsible for self motivation.
5. monitors own progress.
6. works at own speed.
7. chooses when to be assessed.
8. chooses how to be assessed.
9. develops own learning and study strategies.
10. sets own learning goals.

My 'best advice': 1. ....

2. ....

✶ ✶ ✶ ✶ ✶ ✶

Group A note advantages
Group b note disadvantages
Score (a–c)

b) **How to Encourage Learner Independence.**
Advice

1. Initiate 'learner diaries'.
2. Negotiate 'learner contracts'.
3. Set up self assessment procedures.
4. Concentrate classroom focus on the 'process' rather than the product of language learning.
5. Facilitate the internet and computer assisted language learning.
6. Develop learner study groups and peer- support groups.
7. Lower the amount of extrinsic motivation from the teacher.
8. Increase the intrinsic motivation in the tasks and materials themselves.

My 'best advice': 1. ....

2. ....

English Experience, 25 Julian Road, Folkestone, Kent CT19 5HW

TEACHER DEVELOPMENT RESOURCE BOOK

3: COPE WITH BEING OBSERVED.

Group A note advantages
Group b note disadvantages

Score (a–c)

a) Before Being Observed.
Advice
1. Ask to be observed BEFORE they ask you.
2. Identify an area you feel weak on. Ask the observer to focus only on that.
3. Ask for a tutorial with the observer, and incorporate his/her ideas into your observed lesson.
4. Type your lesson plan.
5. Have a long section on anticipated problems in your lesson plan.
6. Try out the lesson on another class first.
7. Pre-teach a lot of the observation lesson's target language the day before the observation.
8. Tell students not to ask you any hard questions during the observation.
9. Tell the students that you'll be observed.
10. Prepare everything beforehand on OHP transparencies.
11. Find out the observer's pet likes and hates.
12. Have a comfy seat, paper and a decent pen prepared for the observer.
13. Ensure a pre-observation chat and find something to compliment the observer on.

My 'best advice':
1. ....
2. ....

✱ ✱ ✱ ✱ ✱ ✱

Group A note advantages
Group b note disadvantages

Score (a–c)

b) During The Observation.
Advice
1. Don't do anything that you can't easily justify afterwards.
2. Use the board as little as possible.
3. Don't raise your voice.
4. Introduce the observer to the students.
5. Cram in a bit of pair, group, individual and class work.
6. Have lots of self-correction and peer-correction from the students.
7. Don't explain anything. Have peer-teaching going on instead.
8. Use edible realia which the observer can try.

My 'best advice':
1. ....
2. ....

✱ ✱ ✱ ✱ ✱ ✱

Group A note advantages
Group b note disadvantages

Score (a–c)

c) The Post-Observation Chat.
Advice
1. Buy the observer a coffee. Bring out the cookies.
2. Have your own evaluation of the lesson prepared in note form.
3. Say what could have gone better, and what steps you could take to ensure this next time.
4. Ask for another observation.
5. Never resist criticism or you'll look defensive, and may attract further criticism.
6. Rephrase any criticism and repeat it back to the observer in a pensive way, to show you value their opinion.
7. If you don't think that the observer's criticism is justified, explain how you will correct the false impression she has got.
8. Don't give the observer feedback on her performance as an observer (unless it's positive).

My 'best advice':
1. ....
2. ....

English Experience, 25 Julian Road, Folkestone, Kent CT19 5HW

TEACHER DEVELOPMENT RESOURCE BOOK

There are 4 **'Smart Alec'** games. The aims are:

Game 1: To encourage teachers to share and value their professional knowledge on **teaching young learners**.

Game 2: To encourage teachers to share and value their professional knowledge concerning **the equipment and teaching aids** that they use in the classroom.

Game 3: To encourage teachers to share and value their professional knowledge concerning **the introduction and production of new language**.

Game 4: To encourage teachers to share and value their professional knowledge on **a variety of issues**.

Instructions for all **Smart Alec** games.

Game Plan.

Play in groups of 4 or 5. Each group will need a 'board', a die, and about 20 'Smart Alec Cards' (see below).

i) Players roll a dice and use counters to make their way round the board.

ii) Each time a player lands on a box marked **SA** the other participants must give plausible advice concerning the statement in that box. The player gives a **'Smart Alec'** card from the pile to the participant whose advice he thinks is best.

The player with the most **'Smart Alec'** cards at the end of the game wins.

N.B. The board also contains other instructions including some which will award more **'Smart Alec'** card (or cause them to be forfeited!)

* * * * * *

Variations

i) Before playing participants play the game according to the Game Plan but the person who lands on a SA square has to propose a solution and the other players award him/her up to 3 'Smart Alec' cards for the answer.

ii) Participants brainstorm what essential advice they would give to a beginning teacher in relation to the topic of the chosen board game. They then discuss the validity and relevance of that advice. At the end of the game, they discuss what they have learned from the other participants.

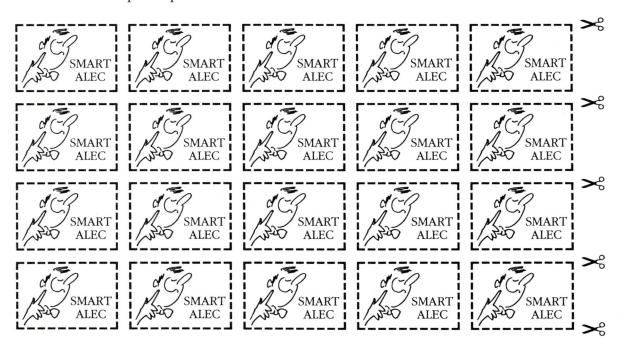

English Experience, 25 Julian Road, Folkestone, Kent CT19 5HW

TEACHER DEVELOPMENT RESOURCE BOOK

1: YOUNG LEARNERS. Game Board.

SMART ALEC

36.	35. **SA** You impose all classroom rules, rather than discuss and negotiate them. Go back to box 9.	34. **SA** My classroom's always a mess with games, toys and materials.	33.	32.	31. **SA** I'm worried about when and how to test young learners without demotivating them.	
25. **SA** I'm in two minds about whether to smack a child, even though I know his parents would approve.	26. **SA** I'd like to give kids a choice of activity but I fear losing control.	27.	28. **SA** I never know when I should introduce the children to writing.	29. **SA** You swap activities and ideas with other teachers at monthly workshops. *Take 2 Smart Alec cards.*	30. **SA** I neither want to inhibit kids nor leave them with the impression that something's right when it's not.	
24. You ensure that each activity is intrinsically motivating. Move on to box 27.	23. **SA** I can never get jigsaw reading and listening activities to work with younger children.	22. **SA** I always seem to be 'on the go' in children's classes and it's wearing me out.	21.	20. **SA** My young learners class is mixed ability.	19. **SA** My classroom has been equipped, furnished and laid out for adults.	18.
13.	14. **SA** I don't know whether to use a lot of TPR (Total Physical Response) activities or whether it's more important for children to speak.	15. **SA** You see English for children primarily as an academic subject. *Lose 1 Smart Alec card.*	16. **SA** One of my young learners is always distracted and fidgets.	17. **SA** While the parents want the children to use the Course book, the kids want to play in English instead.		
12. **SA** The old PPP (Presentation, Practise, Production)) sequence seems inappropriate with young learners.	11. **SA** You save time by getting students to take the register. *Collect 2 Smart Alec cards.*	10. **SA** I don't feel that I'm an English teacher if I focus the kids' attention on the activities themselves rather than on the language they need to complete them.	9.	8. **SA** A child is misbehaving but I don't want to involve the parents.	7. **SA** You avoid activities which overlap the children's other school subjects. Science, Maths etc. *Lose 1 Smart Alec card.*	
1. START	2. **SA** Children don't pay attention when I read the class a story.	3.	4. You subscribe to a monthly periodical on teaching young learners. *Move to box 11.*	5. **SA** The children make it clear that they're in class due to parental pressure not because they want to be there.	6. **SA** I can't get some kids to speak in English, and I don't know how long to respect their right to silence.	

FINISH

English Experience, 25 Julian Road, Folkestone, Kent CT19 5HW

TEACHER DEVELOPMENT RESOURCE BOOK

2: EQUIPMENT AND TEACHING AIDS.   Game Board.

36.	**35.** You don't let students control the equipment. Go back to box 9.	**34. SA** There's unhealthy competition among the teachers to produce the best posters, charts and visuals.	**33.**	**32.**	**31. SA** I am conscious of using aids just for the sake of it rather than because they are really necessary.	
FINISH	**26. SA** Authentic board games are too time-consuming to be used in the class.	**27.**	**28. SA** Adult learners feel it's babyish to use art and creative expression activities in class.	**29. SA** You use visual aids to focus the students' attention and stimulate their imaginations. *Take 2 Smart Alec cards.*	**30. SA** I'm always covered in chalk or board marker.	
25. SA I want to do a jigsaw listening activity but there's only one tape recorder.	**24.** You ask students bring their pocket personal stereos to use in class. *Move on to box 27.*	**23. SA** Realia is too expensive for regular use.	**22. SA** I don't use the board much as I can't control the class with my back to it.	**21.**	**20. SA** Authentic video tapes are too long and difficult.	**19. SA** There's a limit on the number of photocopies I'm allowed to make.
	13.	**14. SA** I'd like to use Cuisenaire rods but I don't know how.	**15. SA** You only use posters and pictures in kids classes. *Lose 1 Smart Alec card.*	**16. SA** My flash cards get tatty and dog-eared almost immediately.	**17. SA** I lost the place on the tape in the middle of a listening lesson.	**18.**
12. SA I never know when to write language on the board.	**11.** You set up and test all the equipment before the students arrive. *Collect 2 Smart Alec cards.*	**10. SA** I can't draw so I don't.	**9.**	**8. SA** My students copy everything I put on the board whether it's necessary or not.		**7.** You put everything on the board in capital letters. *Lose 1 Smart Alec card.*
1. START	**2. SA** My board work is messy and cluttered.	**3.**	**4.** Your sometimes record the students. *Move to box 11.*	**5. SA** I'm unsure about how computers can be exploited for language learning.		**6. SA** Authentic video tapes are too long and difficult for students.

SMART ALEC

English Experience, 25 Julian Road, Folkestone, Kent CT19 5HW

TEACHER DEVELOPMENT RESOURCE BOOK

3: INTRODUCING AND USING NEW LANGUAGE. Game Board.

SMART ALEC

Box	Content
1.	START
2. SA	The school recommends using the old PPP (Presentation, Practice, Production) plan, but that doesn't work when the language isn't totally new to the students.
3.	
4.	You give groups of students sufficient information to work out the rules and meaning for themselves. Move to box 11.
5. SA	If I can't answer all the questions that students ask me about language, I feel I don't know my subject.
6. SA	It takes so long to focus on and analyse new language with the class, that I don't have enough time for practice activities.
7.	Students have to repeat model sentences before they understand the meaning of what they are saying. *Lose 1 Smart Alec card.*
8. SA	I don't know how to make drills interesting, communicative and purposeful.
9.	
10. SA	I never know whether to use the L1 or not to clarify new language.
11.	Pairs of students sometimes research, prepare and peer-teach new language to the class. *Collect 2 Smart Alec cards.*
12. SA	I can't think up good concept questions "off the cuff" in class.
13.	
14. SA	I've never been able to use the Test-Teach-Test sequence successfully.
15.	The choice of new language is never negotiated with students or tailored to their needs. *Lose 1 Smart Alec card.*
16. SA	Students often resent having to work out meaning or rules, for themselves as it takes so long.
17. SA	My students seem to have a wide variety of different learning styles.
18.	
19. SA	I'd like to use authentic texts to contextualise new language but they never contain enough examples.
20. SA	I want the students to research and peer-teach new language but they don't have sufficient reference materials.
21.	
22. SA	I'm never sure of the approach I should take to error correction when students are using new language for the first time.
23. SA	My students want and expect a teacher-centred presentation of new language.
24.	You gather student feedback on how your learners would like language introduced in the classroom. *Move on to box 27.*
25.	
26. SA	My principal expects me to introduce some thing new every lesson, but I'm afraid I'm overloading students.
27.	
28. SA	Despite asking them not to, my students **still** look up new words in their bi-lingual dictionaries.
29.	You vary your approach to cater for the diverse learning styles of your learners. *Take 2 Smart Alec cards.*
30. SA	The activities I design for learners to use new language seem contrived and artificial.
31. SA	I don't know whether to teach technical terms such as 'gerund', and 'infinitive'.
32.	
33.	
34. SA	I never know what aspects of a new word to teach. e.g. synonym, register, affixes etc.
35.	You place great store on learning new language by heart. Go back to box 9.
36.	FINISH

English Experience, 25 Julian Road, Folkestone, Kent CT19 5HW

TEACHER DEVELOPMENT RESOURCE BOOK

4: ADVISING ON TEACHING.   Game Board.

SMART ALEC

1. START
2. **SA** I knowingly gave a student a wrong explanation.
3.
4. You picked up some great tips at the IATEFL conference. *Move to box 11.*
5. **SA** I lost my temper in class.
6. **SA** In class, I keep on rubbing it in that my English is better than my students.
7. You think experimentation is just for inexperienced teachers. *Lose 1 Smart Alec card.*
8. **SA** I keep on repeating what my students say.
9.
10. **SA** I repeat everything that I say.
11. You plan lessons with, and observe other teachers. *Collect 2 Smart Alec cards.*
12. **SA** I don't give students a chance to answer. Instead, I answer my own questions!
13.
14. **SA** My students are sometimes afraid to speak in class, because I correct them too much.
15. You rarely speak up at staff meetings. *Lose 1 Smart Alec card.*
16. **SA** I don't like pair / group work as I don't like students to make mistakes that I can't correct.
17. **SA** It's important to teach British culture, whether the students think it's important or not.
18.
19. **SA** I usually sit behind my desk in class.
20. **SA** I ask students: Do you understand?
21.
22. **SA** I avoid teaching students about regional accents.
23. **SA** I avoid teaching pronunciation.
24. You gather and act on student feedback at least once a month. *Move on to box 27.*
25. **SA** I prefer students to do writing tasks individually in class.
26. **SA** I discourage peer-explanation, as they always get it wrong and I have to explain it again.
27.
28. **SA** Underlining student's mistakes and asking for a second draft of written homework, rarely works.
29. You're conscious of a specific teaching problem and ask a colleague to observe you. *Take 2 Smart Alec cards.*
30. **SA** A controversial remark I made in a class debate upset some students.
31. **SA** I don't ask students about what they want in class as I'm scared they'll criticise me.
32.
33.
34. **SA** The class is so noisy that other teachers complain.
35. You haven't taken a professional development course for 2 years. Go back to box 9.
36. FINISH

English Experience, 25 Julian Road, Folkestone, Kent CT19 5HW

MY GOALS!

Aims To help teachers to set goals and break them down into manageable stages.

In particular: **Example game** – Teaching Speaking Skills

Game 1 – Teaching Reading and Listening
Game 2 – Professional and Personal Growth
Instructions for the 2 **MY GOALS!** games.

Game Plan.   Suggested timing: 60 minutes

i)   Participants put down any goals that they think appropriate to their teaching situation in **My Goal Chart(s)**. It doesn't matter if some seem a bit far-fetched!
ii) Mingle in order to compare and justify their goals.
iii) When players find someone with a similar goal in one of the categories, they should agree on how to achieve it and make notes in the table provided.
iv) In groups of four, participants evaluate and compare each other's tables
v)   Finally, read and evaluate the **ACE Teacher's Goal Chart (or in the case of the very last activity the "Jaded Teacher's" goal chart.).**

Variation Participants discuss the practicalities, viability and the pros and cons of goal-setting in relation to their own teaching situation.

My Goal Chart

Example for **TEACHING SPEAKING SKILLS.**

	Cultural differences in the way people interact.	Talking time.	Fluency.	Register and appropriacy.	Common conversational routines.	Negotiating meaning.
GOALS	To encourage students to be able to turn-take and interrupt as British native speakers do.	To increase the amount for each student.	To decrease inhibition and hesitancy.	To sensitise learners to the need for appropriate register according to the situation and participants.	To teach learners how to greet and leave-take effectively and naturally.	To reduce dictionary and L1 use, and encourage learners to ask questions and use other strategies to work out what their partner means.
HOW TO ACHIEVE THEM	*Analyse authentic videos and discuss in class.*	*Shift from teacher presentations to a guided discovery approach to the introduction and analysis of new language.*	*Find cognitively challenging activities which are intrinsically motivating.*	*Use activities which focus on misunderstandings and negative repercussions which can arise from using inappropriate register.*	*Focus on set phrases and predicting responses in common routines.*	*Negotiate class rules for oral fluency activities and teach set phrases which will help them negotiate effectively.*

TEACHER DEVELOPMENT RESOURCE BOOK

MY GOALS 1: *TEACHING READING AND LISTENING.*

Aim: To help teachers analyse the different aspects involved in teaching reading and listening. To encourage teachers to set goals and break them down into manageable stages.

My Goal Chart

	Type of Text	Students' reading and listening outside class	"Pre-reading" and "Pre-listening" tasks	"While-reading" and "While-listening" tasks	"Post-reading and Post-listening" tasks	Other
GOALS						
HOW TO ACHIEVE THEM						

- - - - - - - - - - - ✂ - - - - - - ✱ ✱ ✱ ✱ ✱ ✱ - - - - - - - - - - - -

An example – the ACE Teacher's Goal Chart!

	Type of Text	Students' reading and listening outside class	"Pre-reading" and "Pre-listening" tasks	"While-reading" and "While-listening" tasks	"Post-reading and Post-listening" tasks	Other
GOALS	Use authentic materials	Ensure it exceeds the amount of exposure they get in the classroom itself	Ensure that I tap into and awaken the students' background knowledge concerning the types of characters in narratives.	Use authentic tasks.	Ensure that the information gathered in the "while-reading" or "while-listening" task is used in a purposeful way.	
HOW TO ACHIEVE THEM	*Create a topic-based file of authentic texts with varied types of input including descriptive, narrative and abstract texts.*	*Project work as part of the assessment system.*	*Match photos, lifestyles, daily diaries and personality descriptions to characters from the texts.*	*Conduct a needs analysis to find out what tasks students (will) need to perform in English and sensitise students to the features of authentic texts.*	*Have students compile and grade a list of their favourite classroom activities.*	

English Experience, 25 Julian Road, Folkestone, Kent CT19 5HW

MY GOALS!

TEACHER DEVELOPMENT RESOURCE BOOK

MY GOALS 2: GENERAL. **Aim:** To help teachers plan for professional and personal growth through breaking goals down into manageable stages.

My Short-term Goal Chart: By the end of this month....

	Teaching.	Work Relationships.	Salary.	Teaching Materials/ Equipment.	Creative Self-Expression.	Leisure/Travel.
GOALS						
HOW TO ACHIEVE THEM						

My Long-term Goal Chart: By the end of this year....

	Teaching.	Work Relationships.	Salary.	Teaching Materials/ Equipment.	Creative Self-Expression.	Leisure/Travel.
GOALS						
HOW TO ACHIEVE THEM						

And finally A Jaded Teacher's Goal Chart: By this time next year....

	Teaching.	Work Relationships.	Salary.	Teaching Materials/ Equipment.	Creative Self-Expression.	Leisure/Travel.
GOALS	To work less.	To have a romance!	To dramatically increase my income.	To have enough material at home so I don't have to prepare lessons at school.	To be more physically dynamic in the classroom.	To get longer paid holidays.
HOW TO ACHIEVE THEM						

English Experience, 25 Julian Road, Folkestone, Kent CT19 5HW